SPECIAL REPORT

Ultimate Guide

To Being a

High Paid **Consultant**

How to Create a Million Dollar
per Year Consulting Business

By Steven Wiellder

Table of Contents

Introduction

Well Hello! You just bought this book, so consider this your first step to increasing your net worth and that's more than what most have done, but before we go any deeper, I would like to insert a small legal disclaimer that my results are not typical, and before we go any further, I would like to make you understand that everyone will have different levels of success with consulting, depending on your skill set, how motivated you are, how hard you work and I can go on and on so many variables. But let's looks at the big picture set your goals and go for it, and hopefully, you can achieve what I have or much more.

Chances are I don't know you, and we probably have not met, so I am not going to promise you or make any claims that you or anyone will be able to duplicate my exact results, I am a highly motivated individual with a varied skill set in business. But anyone can achieve incredible success in this business and create a life altering income to possibly quit

1

your 9 to 5 job punching that clock every day making the big man upstairs rich. Make yourself rich or at least independent so you can walk into your boss's office and tell him you quit.

I am going to show you exactly what worked

for me, exactly what makes me six figures on a monthly basis and it's my genuine desire that you will be able to take what you will be able to learn in this book and utilize some of this information to achieve your goals and dreams.

> I'm going to show
>
> you the ropes and
>
> how it worked for me

Consulting is a real business it requires hard work and even long hours sometimes a substantial commitment to make it work. So if you're the type of person looking for a quick get rich solution that you typically see online, then this is not it.

BUT - if on another hand you are a go-getter, motivated and want to create a true lasting business with an income then this could be for you. If you've got some skills, and the ability to help others and their business, the willingness to work for hard for what you

want, this just might be for you.

In 2015, my business was averaging just over $120,000.00 per MONTH that's right I sad per month most people would be ecstatic if they could make that in a year, never mind a month in revenue. I have two virtual assistants that help me from the Philippines, they work for incredibly cheap, and 80% of my work is done from my home office in New York City. With nothing more than a laptop, a printer, a few pens and a notepad to take notes and my phone that's it.

In this book, I am going to show you how I did it and give you a plan that you can also use to build your 6 figure consulting business.

Why you! Will you Make A lot Of Money in Consulting

If you look at the consulting business the only way to describe the potential is just wow it's a total cash cow no buts or ifs.

Aside from my personal experience in this industry for the last seven years, there are many other reasons. Ok, let's take a look at just a few stats on the consulting business. First, there's the huge amount of money being spent on consulting right now. According to Forbes, consulting is a $100 billion per year industry. That's an astronomically large number, and all you need is a small chunk of that yearly business to make yourself a very comfortable living. I am doing it, and it wasn't hard to get started you would be surprised how many businesses are out there ready to cut you a check every month.

Here's why that's Forbes number is so important...You probably think IT; software is where all the money is, internet marketing or other industries. I hear it every day oh this is hot, and that is the next hot thing to get into.

Listen to this, according to market research, "Internet Marketing" is a $19 billion dollar industry now we can't exactly throw that number under the bus that's a huge number as well, but in terms of comparison to consulting, it's not even close.

If we looks at what small business spends on direct mail every month and yes that includes all the junk mail you get piled up in your mailbox every week. That figure was not a just a walk in the park either at $48 billion a year, So are you starting to see the picture now how big the consulting business actually is. As a whole, people or businesses are spending more on consulting than both Internet marketing and direct mail advertising as a whole put together. Makes you think, doesn't it?

Now I am going to ask you which business would you rather be involved with? In an "economic downturn" or in a $100 BILLION dollar per year industry that's doing nothing but growing by leaps and bounds?

But hold on that's not all! Consultants can also experience another thing most people miss out on Very high net profits compared to my expenses and time involved in this business my cost of doing business with my client's vs. my net profit is small in comparison to most traditional business. At least that's what my experience has been in consulting.

The one thing that I love about this business and makes it so profitable is the low overhead. You don't need a fancy big office, you don't need big servers, or an office staff of twenty people, no fancy equipment just the very basics.

> Consulting can be
>
> very profitable if
>
> you set everything
>
> up right

A home office or your kitchen table will Work just fine, so no rent to pay every month. A laptop or desktop but laptop is preferred so you can take your files with you anywhere.

You will require a phone, so with that, you will have a monthly cost there, but which is very minimal, there are some fixed marketing costs, but that's really it, no significant overhead, and really that's all you basically need. If you set yourself up right, you can have a very profitable consulting business. With minimal operating costs.

8 Fabulous Reasons why you should get into Consulting

Let's take a close look at what you currently do , the fact of the matter is , if you are in the marketing business, online business selling anything, especially such things as "How to " information, eBooks, online courses, affiliate marketing, classes, products and membership sites you really need to consider getting into consulting.

Consulting tends to be much more profitable with one hell of a lower overhead than most of the business that were mentioned above. Let's take a look seven excellent reasons why this is true:

#1: *Recurring Monthly Income:* What most people think or have an understanding of how consulting works, probably not what you imagine. The truth is far from what you're probably thinking. Most people think consulting is done on an hourly basis.

My consulting business and what is going to be taught to you in this book is that I don't set my business up in a paid by the hour format. I am going to show you how to set up your consulting business the right way and how to build your business up in a way that it will provide you with an excellent recurring monthly income month after month.

All my clients pay me month to month, and it's always been that way. Now, what does this mean for you? Well, it means that you don't have to always chase after new clients every month, unless you are totally motived to build and grow your business then you might want to continue to pursue new business or clients.

I don't have to resell new stuff every month just to maintain my current monthly revenue. Most people that sell some sort of product, eBooks or info products have to keep driving new sales running after, another sale every month so there revenue does not drop that month. And guess what if you can't sell anything that month you make zero for the month.

> ## My clients always
>
> ## pay monthly

The beauty of this business is I never worry; my checks arrive in the mail every month from my clients. In 2015 I averaged $120,000.00 month after month.

Another beneficial reason is most clients will stay with you for a long time especially if they are getting great results from your service. So I don't need allot of clients either because of this reason.

So if this type of business sounds like something that's interesting to you, then keep on reading this book because you will discover exactly how you can achieve the same results, and set yourself up the right way, from day one. You can't beat that.

Another huge bonus allot of people to get into consulting for is simply for the reason of predictability, and never really having to stress out about, or where your next paycheck is going to come from, predictable money every month is a great position to be in. It's one less stressful thing that you have to worry about in your life every month. Have you ever been to an event or baseball game as an example yet your mind is somewhere else, and it's not the baseball game? Worrying yourself sick about where your next dollar is going to come from, and how you're going to cover your bills.

In my model, I am going to show you in this book, how to build a small client list that pays you to allot of revenue every single month. This is a model that keeps your customers euphoric. Therefore, they pay you every month, keeping you happy and stress-free, so everyone ends up a happy camper

#2: *SPEED:* To get up and running with consulting takes no time at all even with a semi-focused approach as I took when I first started yet I was still able to bring my business of consulting from zero to $120k a month within about four months' time. What other business can you scale up so quickly with that amount of income per month?

What that means for you is that you do not need to go out and find or create a bunch of products, or set up a brick and mortar location, no need to set up huge mailing lists and even set up sales funnels, etc.

It was straightforward all I did was went out and found some business or people that needed my consulting services; I helped them with their requirements and I got paid nothing more.

I am going to show you how you can get started today, contacting new prospects to start building a business today not waiting three months from now when you have everything set up to start, this model would be another typical way most business start, you would need to go out and set up a brick and mortar location and that takes months , if you were running an online business typically you would have to build huge email lists that takes a lot of time month even years, or create products, these are setbacks that take a long time to prepare before you can even get up and running never mind even making a return on your investment for possibly months after you start your new business .But the good news is, with consulting start up speed is on your side you can start today!

#3: FREEDOM: I think that one of the most beneficial aspects of having your own consulting business is freedom. Why create a business for yourself that you are trading your time, your 40 hour work week for money. If you don't have freedom with your new business, then you just created a job and not a business. Freedom to me means that I am not trading my 40 hour work week for money and compromising my freedom, where I am doing nothing but spending countless hours working for my business, in most cases, it's usually much more than 40 hours per week, typically new ventures require long hours with no freedom. To get up and running, maintaining and chasing after that new dollar every month takes up allot of your time so that your revenue does not diminish. Get my point?

My hours with the consulting business are usually from 8:00 am until noon on Monday through Friday, yes you heard me right, and those are my normal hours.

This is a fact I am working part time hours and earning full-time income does not get much better than that, and if I need to take any time off or only work a couple of hours on any specific day because I need to take the kid to a baseball game. All I do is let my clients know in advance that I won't be available within a time slot and it's no big deal. This is a truly part-time business.

I love this business for the tremendous amount of flexibility and freedom that you have. I am going to show you how you too can achieve a consulting business with part-time hours, full-time pay, and ultimately being worry free with more time to spend with your loved ones or on your hobbies and fun things you enjoy in life. What's the point of having a business that gives you no time to truly enjoy freedom, and what all the beautiful things life has to offer?

#4: HIGH NET PROFITS: We have already covered the fact that a low overhead and minimal starting cost means more revenue for you every month. I am going to teach you how you can structure your business so that not only are you bringing in net profits every month, but also keeping your low fixed costs down every month.

Let's take a look at it this way. You start your business from your home office that means you're not paying rent for a fancy office. I have a dedicated phone line for my business, but you can just use your cell phone. I pay for a virtual employee, but you don't need that either when you start or advertising I rarely even do that much anymore. And once you build your business to the point where you have enough customers you won't need to advertise either.

So because we are not spending much on Marketing on our consulting business, don't, and the fixed costs of operation are very low or minimal, that means the majority of the

14

revenue you make is all in your pocket. That means more spending money for you to spend on vacations, cars homes, or even charity. The money you make is yours and majority of it is not going into overhead like allot of the typical business.

> Most of the revenue
>
> that comes in goes
>
> straight into your
>
> pocket

#5: LOW TECH BARRIER OF ENTRY: Consulting is perfect for anyone who is not tech savvy or someone who doesn't understand how to leverage the power of tech online to make money. If you know how to check your email that's about as tech savvy as you require for this business. You don't need to deal with anything that is very overly technical, I also have a landing page that I collect emails from people who are possibly interested in my service, and I have a PDF that I send out to them, and a follow-up emails its very tech simple for anyone. And we will get into these details in later chapters of this book.

On Occasion, I will do a live webinar to acquire some new consulting clients. By occasion, that usually means I do webinars usually twice a year. It's a basic business model that is not complicated at all. Anyone can do this even without any major tech knowledge.

All the overwhelming, what you may believe in starting this business is complicated and its freaking you out right now, it's so not true with this business, and you never have to worry about it with being a high paid consultant, and if by chance you do find anything to tech savvy for you, just hire someone off Upwork.com or even Fiverr.com for a very cheap price. Some of these services can start as cheap as $5 on these websites.

#6: LOWER STRESS: It's tough to enjoy anything in life if you are under significant stress. It's been studied that stress does kill, it's the silent killer, and if it doesn't kill you, it will eventually cause some sort of chronic illness and destroy your life. There is no better business that you can start that not only is stress-free but gives you all the freedom in the world, so the typical stress factors are wiped out. Most people in new businesses are always

stressing about making enough money to pay next month's rent, -and make enough money to cover all their bills, food, shelter, etc. On top of that stress, they also worry about the business failing if they don't sell enough product or made enough sales for the month. In consulting these stress factors are nonexistent for the most part.

7#: *MUCH HAPPIER CLIENTS:* When you work with your customers directly in this fashion such as I explained earlier. Interacting with them on a personal level, helping them or their business, and not through some online course, your clients will see results much faster. And guess what? Because of this they will be much happier customers, and seeing results they will continue to do business with you for a long time, that's why you don't need many clients. So all you really need is to get yourself from, a few, to a handful of client's and that's all you're going to need. We will figure out how many clients you really need to run your consulting business; we will cover these details in just a few minutes.

The fact of the matter is because you only need a few clients you can also be very selective as to whom you choose as your clients.

#8: CONSULTING IS MUCH EASIER OF A SELL:
Lastly let's take a look at the final reason... why consulting is by far simpler to sell than any other product that you can be possibly selling online or anywhere else. I am going to show you the reason why and it's because of a theory called the **"ladder of desire."**

Let me explain when a person usually buys an Ebook, some sort of class, info product or someone pays you for consulting; they are after a very specific result got me? Well, this is how it works on this ladder of desire. Let's get into this in the next chapter.

> Consulting is much
>
> easier to sell than
>
> most other products
>
> or services.

The Ladder of Desire Explained

"The Ladder of Desire" what does this mean? In simple terms, it explains the form of desire a person has for a particular thing into three broad categories. As you climb up the ladder, that person's intensity of desire keeps increasing. Simply put, both the price tag of the item and the personal involvement also goes up.

It a rare occasion when I client contacts who knows, and is able to express precisely what they want from you as a consultant. Usually, there's some form of shopping around, exploration or asking allot of questions. See if you can estimate or figure out what level they are on in the ladder of desire first because this is going to help guide the conversation going forward with your new client.

Ok, let's~~Let's~~ review the three different types of services sold in the online info world, in terms of teaching people how to achieve there desired results. All three of these services represent a level on the ladder of desire.

LEVEL #1 IN DESIRE: Just Read the "How-to EBook."

Let's start with the least desirable results that we are looking for, the first level of desire, the most simple, less valued, as an example let's say it's a manual or eBook. We can offer these to people. Ironically what everyone this is what in the online world is trying to market or sell these days. That is level number one, the bottom level, the level where you're~~your~~ providing info at a very non-personal level but with some minimal value usually, I like to call this the "you only get the manual" offer. But level one is the least desirable product to offer.

Let's look at an example; someone wants to put up a wall in their living room, they want to divide it into two rooms, but they have no idea where to start or how to build this wall in their home. So in your head your thinking "I really need to figure this out so I can save some money." You go online and find a manual on the subject matter of how to build walls. The author sells you this guide, so now you're on your own buddy good luck to you! You go off with your manual, and you struggle to figure things out. People are pressured into these high sales tactics convincing them into buying this level one info product simply because at the moment they have no other alternatives to find a solution

LEVEL #2 IN DESIRE: "Show Me Exactly How to Do It" or "Do it with Me."

Now let's look at the second level, this is one step up from the first level, and it's quite the step up from just throwing a manual in front of you to actually do it with me or show me how it's done.

Let's go back to our example of the building wall This time, instead of you buying the manual, you have a friend that has built a few walls in his time and he is will to come over give you a hand and show you how it's done exactly so that wall goes up pretty fast and you're as happy as can be.

Do you now see the difference in the ladder of desire, to actually have someone guide you through something you're trying to get results for on a personal level? Now you see how that is much more desirable, to have someone walk you through the entire process, making your desired results much easier, stress-free than just throwing the manual at you. In the end, it saved you from slavering over your project, trying to figure out every small detail until your frustrated and stressed out.

It's much easier task to sell a product or service on level two of the desire ladder then level one, for the simple reason that whenever you can make a person's life simple, then you have an easy product to sell, it almost sells its self

LEVEL #3 IN DESIRE: "Just Do It for Me!"

Let's take a look at the final most desirable level, and how it relates to consulting, This level is the pinnacle as far as the easiest to sell in almost all cases and its simple, some people just want it done for them avoid the hassle prevent the stress.

Using our example of building the wall in your home you can just hire a carpenter or a professional to build the wall for you. It will save you time and time is money, it will save you stress and the possibility of making mistakes if you did it yourself.

So for most people, this level of purchase makes the most sense. It's a very easy sale to make. I have seen some cases were level number two can be more desirable than level three, but the norm is if your running your business based on level two and three that's usually the sweet spot. So in other words "show me how" and also a little of "do it for me, " and you hit the perfect spot. Hence where consulting comes into the picture. A combination of the two on the ladder of desire seems to be the perfect combination as far as being the easiest to sell.

Well let's take a look at my particular consulting business as an example I advise my clients on building e-commerce platform and marketing sales funnels and develop winning campaigns, there follow up email marketing, etc. So that's helping my clients on 2nd level.

I not only take them by the hand and show them how it's done, but I also do some of it for them. So it goes something like this when I am instructing my clients... "Here is what I would like you to change on your web page, "this is how I would like you to create an opt-in page", "and what if we offer this thing as bribe to get them to opt in" and "last let's send these follow up emails out in a unique sequence as part of your sales campaign funnel etc." and I will design your entire program for you.

You see that's a combination of level two and level tree combined. On occasion

I'll step up to level 3 and do some work for

them. For example, let's say we're working on email sequence for my client and they say: I wrote this email based on you tow you asked me to do it; "what is your opinion?" normally when they send it over to me I will normally re-write the headlines or re-write part of the script, I will just fix it and send it back to them. This is level number three where I do it for them.

In the consulting business, this is the pinnacle of the ladder of desire, because I'm assisting my clients in getting them much faster results a headache free by doing some of the work for them.

Even though they are going through the process of being educated by me on the power to know how to do it themselves, yet they are truly never entirely independent and still rely on me for a helping hand on long term basis. This is by far the easiest thing to sell to your clients.

Recapping Consulting:

So to end this chapter, let's recap some of the essential points.

- If we look at the ladder of desire,

consulting sits right into the most desirable level. Due to the position on the ladder of desire, this creates a massive opportunity for anyone that is knowledgeable enough to get the results that your clients are after by making their life easier or increase their revenue.

- Consulting is extremely profitable, simply put; it has very low fixed or overhead expenses. You can set up your office from home, a laptop and a legal pad and a free Skype account and you're pretty much set to go. These are basically the tools of the trade.

- You're barrier of entry into consulting is very fast. You don't need to create info products or eBooks, no need to invest in the latest technology, etc. There really should be nothing to slow you down in starting your consulting business other than your motivation factor, how quickly you can get up and running.

- Consulting is a very stable and growing by leaps and bounds every year. Consulting is also a very recurring business, if you use the method of the monthly billing model that I will teach you in this book, you won't really have to worry about continuously chasing after new clients month after month. After working with your clients and you happen to do a great job for them, make their life easier, or increase their revenues, they will be ecstatic with your service, and they're going to stay with you for the long term.

This chapter clearly illustrates why consulting is a massive opportunity in today's market to get involved in, there is not only a tremendous amount of money to be made in this ever growing market. But there is also a huge number of individuals other that are looking for your consulting services to maximize their results, and you can provide that for them.

Part 1: Consulting In Detail – Let me explain

Let's take a look behind the scenes and dig into what consulting really is; there is a lot of misconceptions about what consulting really is, how it works, and what your role can be in this business.

If we look at the actual meaning according to the dictionary, it states that consulting is when "One person provides professional or expert advice to another person."

That's it.

Consulting is not so much as described in the simple explanation in the dictionary; mind you the basic principle is correct. However, there are many myths that surround itself around the consulting business. Knowing these myths all too well, when I first started I had all these myths in my head, hence why it actually took me a while to get started in consulting even though it pondered in my mind for almost a year before I got the ball rolling, simply because I had all these preconceived notions in my head of what this business entailed at the time.

Let's take a look at some of these myths that are probably going through your mind:

Myth #1: Consulting is a complex business for a bunch of guys in three-piece suits sitting in a boardroom, and you're up there going through flip charts or presentation slides, working with huge corporations. You understand the point I am trying to picture here a very professional stiff uncomfortable environment.

Myth #2 That you must have all this training, or you have to go to school to learn to be a consultant, or you need a major diploma from a big school, because it just sounds like this serious, complicated thing to do that only with a major accreditation to be able to be recognized by your clients.

> None of these preconceived notions about consulting are true

Now, these are only a few myths, even though there maybe some of this involved depending on the type of consulting you get into, but for the most part, most of it is a myth.

Types of Consulting

There is just about anything you can think of doing for consulting, and most of it does not include dudes in suits. If you happen to do a search for consulting in Google, you will see so many different types of consulting available out there. Here are some to put a perspective on what you can possibly get into yourself:

Home Staging Consultant
Mortgage Consultant

Clutter Consultant
Skincare Consultant

Legal Nurse Consultant
Philosophic Consultant

Sports Nutrition Consultant
Sales Consultant

Grant Writing Consultant

Postnatal Fitness Consultant

Restaurant Consultant
IT Consultant

Tupperware Consultant
Avon Consultant

Online business backup Consultant
Social Media Consultant

Mary Kay Cosmetic Consultant
Marketing Consultant

Online researcher consultant
Personal Chef Consultantconsultant

Weight Loss Consultant
Art Consultant

Copywriting Consultant
Fitness Consultant

Wedding Consultant
Jury Consultant

Financial Consultant
Small business Consultant

Independent Consultant

HR Consultant

Business Consultant
Graphic design Consultant

CHRP Consultant
Tax Consultant

Now if you do a google search on some of these types of consulting, you will be shocked at the how many million searches are done every month. As an example "productivity consultant" I have trained serval students on this type, there are 27 million Google search results. "Sales consultant," this one should not be much of a surprise, 148 million Google search results. "Dating consultant," yes, that's right 28 million Google search results. The numbers are huge, and demand is enormous.

There are all types of consultants out there in every field you can probably imagine, all you have to do is do a google test. You may be wondering, could I take my knowledge and build a successful consulting practice around my skill set, and the answer is probably yes. It's a very simple way to test this, simply go to Google and type in your area of expertise and type with the word consultant afterward or type in coaching or information advice and you will be surprised at the results that Google will retrieve. If your results come back anything like the examples I have shown you above, then chances are there is a huge market out there for your skill set. The US government says the consulting is set to grow by 83% by the year 2018 you can be part of that huge number, and most of these consulting types do not involve wearing a three piece suit.

Part 2: Factors shouldn't be Holding You Back

You're probably wondering if consulting is so great, how come everybody's brother and uncle are not doing it, why are not more people getting into it? Well in actuality allot of people are now getting into consulting including some big gurus. With job numbers being in the negatives and individuals wanting to start their own business it is growing on daily bases and more and more people are getting into it.

However, the general population is held back due to some factors and not considering consulting? Why? Most people are paralyzed by the credentials myth; they believe they don't have a diploma or credentials they don't have enough knowledge. They believe because they didn't attend a big school and no one gave them the formal credentials as a consultant, therefore how I can be a consultant.

This is understandable and the number one reason people don't follow through with a consulting practice.

The second biggest reason is the belief that if you sell your consulting service the wrong way you're screwed. Any previous idea you had on marketing the typical way that you have learned in the past, you will fail if you use it to get consulting clients. Standard marketing ideas will not work to get consulting clients. We will get into how you get your clients in this report. This is a whole new animal and a different game in terms of obtaining new clients than what you typically believe.

The beauty of this business is you don't have to get into all the sleazy marketing ploys that you would typically need online to get new buyers or clients; you know the stuff that your use to being exposed to online.

Let's look at the credentials myth a little; I know this one very well since I am guilty of this one myself when I got started.

It's a real shame that self-doubt and self-belief hold most people back from moving forward with most ventures, this is a barrier that stands between you and making money or even fortunes for some. You have sabotaged yourself rights from the get go if your mentality is self-doubt. You have to stop listening to that voice in your head, coming up with excuses and doubting yourself of your abilities these thoughts need to be blocked out

Those thoughts that circulate in your mind telling yourself "How dare you think that you could get into consulting?" or "Who are you to be able to consult someone else?" This is nothing but self-doubt sabotaging your success. This little voice in our heads is just a bunch of bull but we can all easily fall prey to this powerful voice in our heads, I know I have experienced it myself.

In the real world you and I both hold power within ourselves to change that, the fact of the matter is if you can help someone

34

achieve a goal faster, better and more efficiently then that's all the credentials you require, you don't need an official diploma on your wall. The results will speak for themselves with your clients.

Let's look at some real world examples of people who achieved great accomplishments in business and other areas of life, which didn't have the credentials to do what they are now doing. I am sure you will know most of these highly accomplished people. Let me introduce you to some of these people who didn't have the credentials. So if that voice in your head has been telling you that you don't have the credentials "how can I possibly do this" then look at the following people that possibly had the same situation as you about credentials.

- You might have heard of this guy who just happens to have made the Windows Microsoft software and computers many years ago. Bill Gates was a college dropout, yes you heard me right one of the richest men on our planet was a college dropout with no credentials before he founded the biggest software computer company in the world Microsoft.

- Another guy by the name of Mark Zuckerberg no fancy credentials for him either, you just know him as the Facebook Dude, Mark Zuckerberg didn't wait for anyone's permission to start Facebook or wait for any technical diploma to start this his multi-billion dollar company.

- How can we not mention Steve Jobs where would we all be in today's world without our iPhones and Apple computers? Steve Jobs has no legitimate credentials at all; he was also a college dropout. He and Wozniak started Apple Computers, and as we all know he changed the world with his devices.

I actually dug deeper into this subject matter and looked up the billionaire's list from Forbes Magazine, believe it, or not, thirty-one of the listed billionaires are all college dropouts, yes that mean no real credentials.

Michael Dell founder of Dell computers, Ted Turner no credentials yet he changed the face of media forever, as the biggest media cable network glamor ant, Kirk Kerkorian, and Lawrence Ellison nothing no credentials.

So the actual fact is this, I know what is going through your mind; I use to have the same mindset. I don't have any diploma and no credentials I barely made it through high school; I had attention disorder when I was in school so most stuff would go in one ear and out the other just as fast. I just barely got all my credits to graduate. So my credentials are really zero.

After leaving high school, I held some mediocre jobs just to survive and eat. I tried being a car salesman for a while after realizing that I was spending countless hours at the dealership and I was not selling many cars; I came to the reality check that I was not the best salesman. I left that and worked in construction for a while eventually left that held a few other really low-level labor jobs in manufacturing plants; I had a ton of self-doubt. I had no education so how could I possibly feel like I could make the big bucks.

Imagine putting my work experiences on a consulting resume? So as you can see I had no real credentials before my life changed and got into the business world and then eventually into consulting. Considering what I like to call negative credentials, I was able to go out and create a very successful business. I was able to remove most of my limiting beliefs out of my mind and move forward, become a consultant and build up a wildly successful practice in a very short amount of time. So, believe me, I get it I been there in your shoes, so the fact is if your freaking out not having credentials just look at where my background came from and how even the richest men in the world had no credentials. So you have absolutely what it takes to start a successful consulting practice.

The bottom line is you can do this! In the modern age of the internet, we can't believe that there must be something that you know that absolutely no one else must know , but the real fact is, you don't need to find something that no one else knows, all you need to know is more than your clients, that it ! It's that simple! All the credentials you need.

All you need to do with your clients is get better faster results than they can on their own, that's all you need, and everyone is happy in the deal.

Your clients, that's what they care about. They are not concerned with what school you attended or what diploma you're holding or what credentials follow your name on your business card. They just don't care. But what they do care about is if you can demonstrate you can get your clients the results there after saving them time and money.And if you can actually provide these results for your client, he will be ecstatic with your services. That's all your client cares about.

The real secret to consulting is a simple formula, is to know more than your client does, period. Nothing else! Who cares what the rest of the world's thinks, they are not giving you a paycheck every week. As long as you can get your clients faster results to achieve their goals and I am going to show you how.

Part 3: What are your Monthly Financial Goals

Goals represent your future without goals how can you picture and materialize what you want in life so before we dig any deeper into this chapter let's talk about goal setting for your consulting business.

I am going to teach you what I know about getting clients, keeping them on board and how to run your consulting business in a successful way. I am also going to show you how to instill confidence in your prospects and then how you can turn them into paying customers in this report.

But before we get to those details, first let's figure out your income goals and what the next steps would be.

I would like you now to take a moment and really think what you're ideal salary would be over the next 12 months, it doesn't matter what the number is but think of a number that you feel would make you happy a number that you feel would leave you financially content.

What would be your early goal? After you have that number in your head, let's divide that into your monthly income goal and figure out what that number would be by dividing your early goal by twelve.

So your monthly goal as an example might be something like this, let's just say that your early goal was $200,000 and we take that number and divide it by twelve, and you get a monthly income goal of $16,666 every month.

Before you get all worked up on these numbers you just created in your head, I am not going to promise you that somehow you will make $200,000 a year or $16,666 a month, nut neither is I saying that your goal should be this number. If your goal number seems too high for you then that fine if it seems too low for you that fine also. However! All the power to you no matter what your financial consulting goal number should be is perfectly fine.

We are only pulling these numbers arbitrarily for the purpose of illustration and to analyze some hypothetical examples. That's all! So this is not really an income claim, I am sure you get it, just wanted to make it very clear.

Ok so let's again take a look at your early goal of say $200,000 a year salary or $16,666 a month, with these numbers we can now look at some comparisons of consulting versus the product route.

Product Route: If you were selling an info product or a physical product in the real typical world, and lets say for examples sake your product cost was $100 for each product, For you to make $200,000 a year selling your physical or info product you would need to sell about 2,000 copies of your one product to make the same salary of $200,000. That's 2,000 people that need to agree to purchase your product, that's quite allot of people that need to agree with their purchase of your product. Now here is the kicker! What I have found from my past experience marketing online with physical and info products is that to get people to agree to buy a $10 product is no easier then to get people to purchase a $5,000 purchase. So if we look at this picture, would you be comfortable at the prospect of going out and trying to sell 2,000 products and getting that many people to say yes over the next year? Days? That's allot of people that have to agree to give you a yes to your products. It's not easy; I know I been there. I also look at the way I use to do things online when I was selling info products. I would be buying traffic, and the average conversion rate was only about 1% of that purchased traffic. So one out of 100 people who came to my website would buy a product via my sales funnel, So if we analyze things that way you would need $200,00 clicks the old school way or product route, and since I was paying a dollar per click, my net profit would be a big zero.

Consulting Route: Ok now let's take a close look at the consulting model vs. the product route, a comparison so you can see how much easier consulting really is compared to the product route. So if we look at the yearly salary earning we discussed early of $200,000, how many real clients would you require a year to generate that amount of income? It's a great question, and the answer is it really depends on your pricing model. I charge my clients always on monthly bases, I don't charge by the day or by the week or based on an hourly rate. I also don't try and get any of my clients into monthly contracts at all. The barrier to entry for my clients is very open, and none committed, so they don't feel like they are obligated for any real length of time. My clients generally stay on board until they are achieving their desired results.

This makes for a very simple approach to selling my consulting services. Basically, the way I approach it is "hey if you want me to help you" this is what I charge per month and you keep working with me until your satisfied with the results, or you don't need my services anymore. It's a very relaxed laid back sale no pressure tactics.

So back to the question of how much you charge, again it all depends, my personal clients are so happy when they see the returns they get that they tend to stay with me for a long time no matter they are paying me.

Now if we look at some hypothetical numbers for the sake of looking at how many clients you really need to achieve your $200,000 a year goal. Keep in mind these are just hypothetical numbers no claims to what your able to make it might be allot more or allot less depends on many factors, your motivation levels, your skill set, how hard you want to work, etc. For the simple purpose of illustration, so what we can see what is possible and some numbers you might want to consider aiming for.

So let's say that you charge your clients $9,000 a month as I do, then you would achieve your goal number of well over $200,000 a year with only three consulting clients on board with you. That would generate approximately $27,000 a month with just three clients that hopefully stay on board with you for a very long time.

- If you charge your clients only $3,500 a month, then you will need five clients to achieve your goals.

- If you charge your clients only $2,500 a month, then you will need seven clients to achieve your goals.

- If you charge your clients only $1,500 a month, then you will need 12 clients to achieve your goals.

Now here's the kicker if we look at the product selling route, it's actually very interesting, to get those twelve clients or sales in that same situation; if your conversion rate was only 1 out of 100 people who entered your sales funnel to get those twelve clients, you would need a whopping 1,200 clicks.

Now, which would you rather try to generate 1,200 clicks or $200,000 of revenue?

As an example let's look at the last campaign, I ran to acquire some new clients I was actually on vacation in Lisbon Portugal, so I decided that I would run a small marketing campaign since I am a workaholic and should have been enjoying my vacation but ended up working while on vacation as well pretty sad! I know!

So to make a long story short, I decided to run an ad on I Facebook PPC those happen to be those small ads on the right-hand side of your profile when you are browsing Facebook seeing what all your friends are up to, those ads that usually have the picture and some sort of catchy. Anyways my ad got me a total of about 5,000 clicks on my ad, from those 5,000 clicks I got about 1,050 leads or opt-ins whatever you prefer to label it, of the 1,050 leads , 12 individuals decided that they wanted to work with me as clients. That's all it took; it's actually more clients than I really need.

As I explained earlier in this book there was no complicated or pushy sales email sequence; no real follow up, it was as simple as, this is what I can offer you! Here is my price, pretty straight forward and simple, do you want to become a client? Bingo! That was it you want to become a client? Great.'

So out of the 1,200 people I had 12 of them say "Yes, I want to become one of your clients." Next question was how much you charge for your service? Let's do business." However the interesting this is before I ran my marketing campaign I was only really looking for three new clients, I had lost a few of my long-term clients, and I need to get a few more to keep my income at my goal level. I actually had no idea that my campaign would work so well and bring me, 12 new clients; the funny thing is I ended up only taking the three clients I was looking for and put the remainder on standby.

The most interesting story in this example of my last campaign is that those 3 new clients I just got from that marketing campaign brought me an income of nice income of about 9,000 each for per month, one client stayed with me for 7 months and paid me $63,000 another stayed with me almost 11 months and paid me $99,000 and the third client stayed with me 8 months and paid me $ 72,000 with a total income for the year of $234,000 just with those 3 clients. That one little Facebook marketing campaign brought me in $234,000 in annual revenue.

Let's just assume that your clients will

stay with you for as long as my clients stay with me usually for an extended period of time as I just shown you; I am going to show you how you can get your clients and keep them on board with you for a long time as well.

And you're not going to be doing this through manipulation or any shady manner, but by doing a great good job for them and keeping them happy.

7-Part Five- Choosing the Right Consulting Clients

Choosing the right clients is essential for your success in the consulting practice before we go any further let's take a look at the right segment of your market if you're not in the right segment of your market you will have a hard time in success with this business.

If we look at the typical consumer, and the different segments of purchasing power of these different segments, you will begin to understand how picking the right clients, in the right segments, can make or break you in this business.

As an example, if you look at consumer electronics particularly high tech electronic gadgets the latest and greatest coolest toys for boys and girls such as MP3 players, smartphones, headsets, blue tooth gadgets etc. I know this really has nothing to do with the consulting business, but we are using this as an example, so you understand the difference between choosing the right clients in the correct segments. These are just hard

49

statistics.

On average the stats of someone that purchases these types of electronic consumer gadgets, according to stats they show that men between the age of 38 to the age of 65 spend on average of about $120 a year on these types of items, however here is the kicker men from the age group of 18-37 spend on average of 300% more than the older age group on the same type of consumer electronic goods. Interesting isn't it? No difference in the goods but a huge difference in the amount of money the younger age group is willing to spend on these items versus the older age group.

So if you look at this example, you can see how you can increase your revenue by 300% just by choosing the right segment or audience of the market.

By saying you need to choose the right segment, or giving you this example to show you how incredibly important it is to realize that, as an example you might be used to selling low-priced products or services to any one section of the market, doesn't mean you need to live in that segment of selling inexpensive items. As I have illustrated in this example of consumer electronics. If the same person targets a younger demographic, you automatically get a huge pay raise just by making this adjustment by slightly changing the age range. So let's look at this a little closer in the next chapters of this book, let's analyze this little closer, so you fully get this concept.

Let's look at it this way. In order for you to do this, I want you to make a decision on what segment of your market is going to benefit the most from working with you.

Who can you help the most right now with your consulting service right now?

The reason this is so essentially important to you is because the segment you decide to get the most and the fastest results for are likely to pay you the most money and usually with the least amount of resistance when it comes to spending money on your consulting service. I know they may sound like it doesn't make any sense or even strange but I'll illustrate it in a minute. Let's see how that is so.

It's way easier for me pick up a new 7-figure client, someone with a million or multimillion dollar business to that will pay my $9,500 per monthly, much easier and makes more sense than it be for me to get a newbie with no business and no product and a business that is not making a million dollars plus a year.

However I would probably advise both clients the same way, it's not like I'm going to give second-rate information to the newbie versus the guy with the 7-figure successful business. Either the newbie or the 7-figure business guy I am dealing with will require the same info great marketing funnels, good product descriptions, and good products, all the stuff I normally help all my clients with.

But the kicker is that it's so much easier for you or me to get the multi-million dollar consulting client to pay my monthly fees than it is a newbie who does not have the money I charge every month. You're probably asking why? Well, the bottom line is, my million dollar plus clients generally speaking already have huge email lists, they have tons of organic Google traffic, there probably already selling great products with high-profit margins. And because this is usually the case, it doesn't take a huge effort to make their business grow or make them more money than they are already making just by taking my knowledge tweaking and consulting them to drive higher sales and more profit for their business.

The reason for that simply is, these businesses have momentum, the reality is these clients have momentum, and that's what you need for your consulting business.

I am trying to set the right mind frame for you here; I want you to really think and set your mind set up for success by only working with the right clients the easy wins for your consulting business.

I don't want to go on about myself, but I am using my personal consulting business model as an example to illustrate how you too can succeed in the consulting business as I have.

In my personal business, I find it very easy for me to keep my clients happy, especially if they already have a successful product with a big mailing list and they are selling an expensive product with great profits. All I've got to do is produce way more than what he is actually paying me, and that makes for a win-win situation between you and your clients, It could be as easy as a phone call tweaking an email he is sending out that we come up with together, probably over the phone. He ends up making five times more than my fee, he is happy, and it all works out for both of us. Hence they stick with me for a long time.

As this example illustrates this is a great easy win scenario win for me when I obtain new consulting clients and even my existing ones. And for the client it is a major win also.

> **Chase the market segment you get the fastest results for, this is Likely to pay you most**

You can absolutely generate the same type of success with your consulting business by creating the same sort of huge profits focusing only on the proper segment of the marketplace that you are chasing.

Here are some keys to correct market selection...

- If you're following my lead and you find the right consulting clients you're not going to need allot of clients to reach your income goals.

- Remember those hypothetical numbers we went over, because of these results you can be very picky. Remember you don't have to work with everybody, just work only with the best people that meet your criteria.

- You need to decide who's going to benefit the most from consulting with you, and benefit the fastest with you, make this your target market. By doing this you will find much less resistance, and much easier to sell your consulting services.

- Finally, make your life much easier by only taking on clients that you can quickly and easily get results for. This will keep your clients happy and eliminates allot of stress on your behalf.

8-Part Six- How to Obtain Clients – the Old Way

So we are finally going to get to the part of the book where I show you how to get clients. I know that's the most important part you are probably waiting to hear about and most likely the reason you even bought this book. So let's get into how to get clients, and that's exactly what I will be delivering here for you.

Keep in mind that we are discussing the consulting model here and it's allot of easier to run and maintain compared to traditionally selling info products physical products online. Always keep that in the back of your head that you do not need allot of clients if you do a great job and they keep paying you monthly.

We discussed the fact that you don't need to make allot of sales in order to do well in this business or matter of fact to be successful in consulting if you follow my advice. Remember that example of only having twelve clients that equates to only twelve total sales that's it. I have already mentioned this many times, if you do a great job for your consulting clients, they will always stay with you for a long time, and that means guaranteed income for you. So because of this, there is no need to keep chasing after new business all the time, no need to constantly add to the pipeline, but it's important that you pay attention and that you approach this business the right way for success.

This approach that you need to take with this business is probably very different than you are typically use to, you have all been on other people's mailing lists and have seen the approach they use to get your dollars from your pocket.

We are all in the same boat and community; we are used to being bombarded by internet marketing promotions, product launches, and affiliate promotions and so forth on daily bases. The reality is almost everything you are used to seeing is almost guaranteed not to work if you try and use these methods with the consulting business.

I will tell you right now if you're going to try to go out and get new clients for your consulting business and you're going to use these typical marketing tactics; I will tell you right now you will likely fail.

Please make sure your paying very close attention to what I am going to cover in the next chapters if you want to succeed in this business and obtain new clients. I want you to say, "this guy repeats himself a lot in this book but holy crap I got myself some clients this guy rocks and really knows his stuff."

So let's take a look at this process much closer, let's make that happen right now. Here's reality. What you and I both are used to seeing on daily bases as far as marketing new products or services is something called the SIGNIFICANCE MODEL.

This is what everyone out there marketing their products is out there doing to you as the consumer. Tell me if what we will be covering here will not sound familiar to you. A new product or service comes onto the marketplace. Its now time for them to get your attention about this new product.

What's the first message you typically see, the product creator tells you how wonderful he is and then followed up by another message telling you how fantastic their product is next?

> Majority of people
>
> don't buy because
>
> who wants to respond
>
> to that type of sales
>
> pitch

This is the same thing you typically see or the equivalency of a guy standing in front of a 10 million dollar mansion with a Ferrari and Lamborghini sitting in front of this home and money falling from the sky, nothing but fantasy.

So the normal step in that marketing funnel goes something like this, "look at me I have all this stuff I am not only saying that I am awesome, but you can with certainty say so because all these other people say I am great also "

Then you get the affiliates that promote the product chiming in and saying, oh yes this guy's extremely great, and you should really believe how wonderful this guy really is, and I am going to make a killing with this guy and so will you if you buy his products, etc. They are basically pumping this guy's products, almost like pumping and dumping stocks.

So the next typical step goes like this "if you want to be great like me, then you need to give me some cash "buy my stuff. People at this point either fall for this sales funnel and buy or don't buy.

Of course, the majority of people don't buy based on these shady sales tactics and funnels, because who wants to buy or even respond to such a shady sales pitch.

So the next phase in the sales funnel is like the following "if you don't buy now there won't be any more product, or the deal ends, etc." They are trying to imply scarcity "listen if you don't give me your money now it's going to be too late." All they are trying to do is called implied scarcity. Something along the lines of "You better order my product right now because we only have limited copies, mind you with downloadable products there is only 100 million copies countless copies available ha-ha. But they always claim there is only so many downloadable copies available and its time sensitive so you better give me your money and get your copy now or it will be too late. This is called the significance model to online marketers.

This whole model is based on "Look at me, look how great I am, how great I am doing, what I have, and what a fabulous big guru I am." Here is the thing about this model, people can sometimes be impulse buyers and fall for this shady ploy but for the most part people see right through this model, and they don't buy for the most part. If you also look at this model and have resented such an approach in the past and don't ever see yourself selling anything like this with such a shady practice, then you're inherently right. Here is why you are right to feel that way. Bottom line this has to be the worst approach period to selling anything. It's an absolute disaster and secondly its very douchey approach to sales.

Think about it this way; imagine if you were doing some sort of sales that involved visiting someone's home, to sell them any sort of physical product be it vacuums or water filters or anything for the sake of this example. So you made an initial call to them to get some interest, and they finally say *"ok sir will you come over and tell us more about what you have to offer*" Could you imagine now showing up for your appointment at their home. And running a sales pitch on them like this: *"Hi, Mr. Smith look at me, Am I not so wonderful, look how great I really am, and look at all my amazing product. Look at how fabulous these other people said I am. Hey, listen Mr. Smith; if you want to be great like me, you need to give me your money. Wait! What? You don't want to give me some cash now? Well, you better give me your money now because the whole world is going to end soon and your days are numbered."*

Think about how ridiculous this would be trying to sell anybody this way; it's absolutely so lame, you would be kicked out on your butt so fast, its plane just douchey. And it doesn't help the client in way or shape either. This douchey approach does not instill any confidence in your client in trusting you whatsoever. The reason for this is because it's all about you, right? And not about how it will better their lives or their business etc. Plus no one wants you to come over to hear about yourself; your clients don't care about you. You have to understand the bottom line is that your clients only care about themselves and more so, they care about getting the results they are after.

You can thank God for that one because it takes away the pressure from you and me as consultants, we don't convince anyone that we are cool or we are so wonderful, all we have to do as consultants is be able to help them with their business that all pretty simple.

So as you can see the guru-centric significance model does not instill any confidence in the clients what so ever so it's not recommended that you take such an approach with them ever. They will have absolutely no confidence in you when you do that douchey sales significance model.

A good friend of mine one of the best online marketers I have ever known once said to me

"The amount of money someone is willing to pay you will be in direct proportion to the amount of confidence they have in your ability to get them results."

Now doesn't that totally make sense in every way? You don't ever want some dude standing in your face giving you shady sales pitch telling you how wonderful he is; therefore you should buy his product. You don't truly believe, or anyone ever believes someone is going to get you results just because your bragging how great you are. No that's not the way it works. The way it really works is the guy would have to say something along the lines of...

"you need some help? Well I have six solutions to solve your problems, well why don't you go ahead and try this, now did this work for you, why don't you try this next? Then hey do you want me to help you do the rest of this?

Considering you just instilled a lot of confidence in your clients by providing this appropriate sales approach, then the amount of money your clients are willing to spend on you is in proportion to your ability for you to get them the results they are seeking. So the big question is how do we build a huge amount of confidence in your clients?

What is the magic bullet, what is the secret to building that confidence in your clients? In the next chapter, we are going to look at this model in detail. I am going to walk you through the client –centric model in the next chapter.

Part 6: How to Obtain Clients – the New Way

The client-centric model, let's see how it works.

First and foremost with this model we never really talk about ourselves much especially how wonderful we are. Why? Because as I have already mentioned your clients could care less about you, all they care about us, if we can get them the results thereafter in their business right? So no bragging about how fabulous we are!

We also don't use any of the typical, online marketing funnels that you're sick of seeing and so are they sick of seeing the same thing on a daily basis. Instead, all we are doing is simply demonstrating we can help their business do more make more money, etc. The beauty of what we do our concept is very novel and simple, by actually helping them, this causes them to pursue us, instead of us chasing them for their business, it's the other way around.

Here is a simple story to illustrate my

point imagine you are in the middle of the bush camping then all of a sudden you hear some noises outside of your tent you're scared but you don't know what it is so you need to come out and see what's outside your tent. So you decide to step out, but all you have is a small knife for protection. To your surprise and fear you are surrounded by a hungry, ferocious pack of timber wolfs, and they are growling and surrounding you wanting to attack and probably eat you , tear you to pieces, but all you have is a small knife to defend yourself, and against a pack of wolfs that won't do much. Then out of the blue, you hear a gunshot and one of the wolfs has been shot the rest run off , a mountain man comes out of the bush holding a massive rifle, he just saved your life

So what first thing that comes out of your mouth? Probably thank you first, then maybe can you kill the rest of those wolfs for me! Well, this is exactly the situation we're going to try to show you in the consulting business.

I am going to show you exactly how to do it, but of course, no wolfs involved in this picture. Here's how it really works in the non-wolf story. We first start with some traffic. We send some traffic to what's called an opt-in page with a very compelling offer. I will fill you in on these details in a minute.

We then follow that up immediately with my seven-step marketing process, which includes what I like to call irresistible intrigue; that then leads to the next step, which is where the possible client or new prospect qualifies himself to you. Then what you do is you turn that prospect into a paying customer by using my collaborative close process and then the client gives you some money you finally get paid.

Now let me show you how to do ~~it~~ this.

Let's get started with getting you some traffic.

Part 7: Getting Traffic for your Consulting Business

There is probably a hundred ways to get traffic out there, However in the consulting business, specifically for my business, I have only really only used three methods, and that has been all I have needed to get more clients than I can actually handle at times.

Here are the three methods I use:

1. **Facebook PPC.** Yes, that's correct I don't mean posting cute pictures of your pets doing tricks or anything like that, Facebook PPC (pay per click ads that people click on). This is basically the same thing as Google AdWords. Facebook puts your ads in front of the right audience, they click through your

ads on the right-hand side of your Facebook page, and you pay per click through. It's very easy, fast to set up. Extremely powerful platform to get traffic on.

2. **LinkedIn PPC.** Is almost like Facebook but for the job world and professional profiles, if you're looking for professional clients and you should be, then advertising on LinkedIn PPC (pay per click) it works just as well as Facebook or Google AdWords.

3. **Direct Mail**. Sounds like an old school method but it works and works very well I personally have done very well using this method it is almost my secret weapon. Most people are abandoning this method but sometimes the old school methods are still on fire and often times more so.

Let's start by looking at Facebook unless you been living under a rock I am sure you have heard of Facebook as has three-quarters of the world's civilized population has.

Facebook has literally changed the world in so many aspects, and as far as the traffic or marketing game Facebook PPC is what Google AdWords use to be back in the day. The name of the game has literally changed with the advent of Facebook

There is just such an enormous potential with Facebook so much you can do, and I don't mean posting cute pics of your vacations or pets, etc. We are talking about advertising here folks; it's the biggest platform for you to advertise on right now, is extremely powerful.

Facebook by far has to be the most targeted platform you can possibly advertise on. Hear this Facebook has partnered up with three of the biggest consumer data providers on the earth to give you absolutely the most advanced targeting ad opportunities that we've ever have available as marketers online. We have never had such targeted audiences not even with Google AdWords as we have now have with Facebook PPC. And all this wonderful targeted marketing with Facebook is Fairley new; this stuff just recently happened within the last few months or so. Facebook has almost always had PPC advertising, but after their partnerships with these data providers, the options on their platform is just unreal.

Check it out!

When you are placing ads on Facebook, you now have the option of choosing data partners by going to the power editor selecting any of these data partners and say:

- Show me anybody that meets these very specific demographics.

- Show me anybody filtered by their level of affluence.

- Show me anybody filtered out by a specific job or purchase history, or even as detailed as the type of automobile they drive.

There are literally more than five hundred new categories like this that have just been added. Here's one example in terms of job roles:

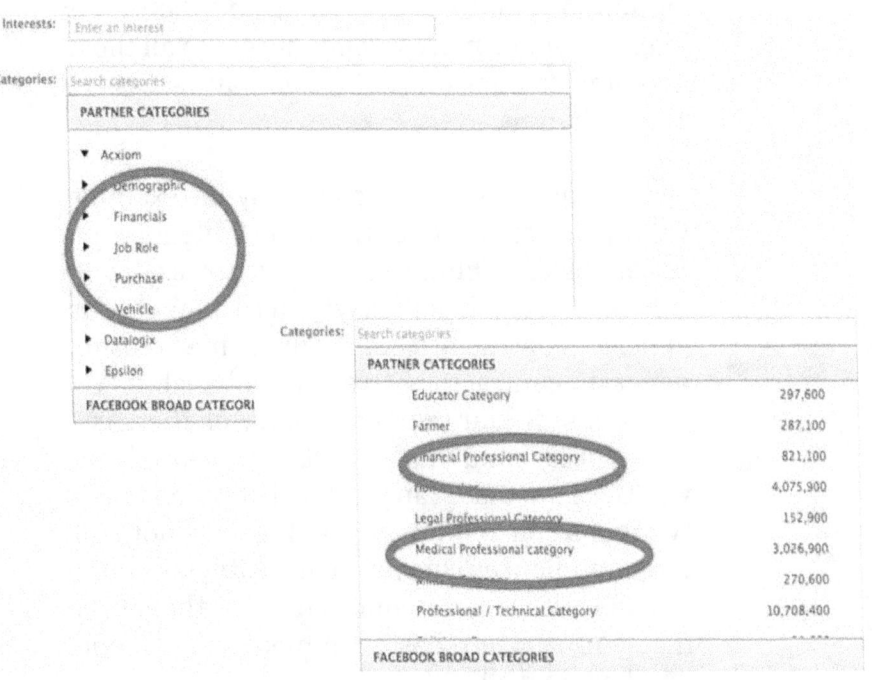

For example, if you wanted to only reach financial professionals only with your ad, well, you would have access to approximately 121,000 of them preselected by Facebook and their partner companies.

Maybe you're looking for medical

professionals, not a problem Facebook's has about three million of those preselected for you and your ad campaigns. There are over literally over 500 categories like these as an option for you to choose from, and the cost is no different or more to have access to all these targeted categories. And we all have access to this right now.

It doesn't stop there let's say for example that you cannot find the right category on Facebooks five hundred plus categories. If you wanted to reach let's say you're looking for general contractors, and for some reason, general contractors weren't available on Facebooks list, or their partners, well there is a nice workaround that as well. This is a website where I go to that I can just buy lists of business types or a consumer type that I find my optimal target audience. This particular site has about 312,000 US general contractors on their lists that you can purchase complete with phone numbers and all.

2013 US Funeral & Crematorium Services Database contains the most up-to-date business records from 26,000+ US Funeral & Crematorium Service Providers. This comprehensive business database can be used for marketing products or services, networking, research or even job seeking. Updated semi-annually. Download Now!

2013 US General Contractor Database contains the most up-to-date business records from 312,000+ US General Construction Contractors (All Levels). This comprehensive business database can be used for marketing products or services, networking, research or even job seeking. Updated semi-annually. Download Now!

2013 US Health Club Database contains the most up-to-date business records from 34,000+ US Gyms, Fitness & Health Clubs. This comprehensive business database can be used for marketing products or services, networking, research or even job seeking. Updated semi-annually. Download Now!

2013 US Home Health Care Service Database contains the most up-to-date business records from 29,700+ US Home Health Care Service Providers. This comprehensive

Now before you think I want you to start calling these phone numbers, I would never want you to ever call these numbers. I would never want you to call somebody out of the blue unless they asked you to call them for more information. But listen up these phone numbers can be very useful to be used within the context of Facebook. Why or how? Well, let me tell you how!

Facebook's got this wonderful tool called custom audience. This tool is just amazing and what it enables us to do with it as far as finding more targeted audiences is just fabulous.

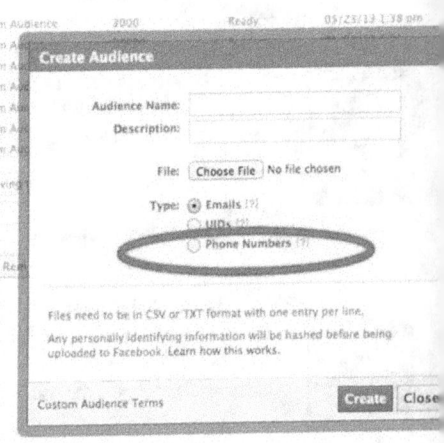

First, we go to that website and purchase a list of let's say those contractors or medical professionals or whatever you choose; it doesn't really matter. We strip out all those numbers, and then you upload those phone numbers into Facebooks custom audience tool.

So what Facebook does next is going out and scrapes its database with anyone with those matching phone numbers, and now you can send your PPC Facebook ads to all those people, it doesn't get any easier or more targeted than that

Ok so let's recap, you buy a list from a site like http://usbizdata.com/ , this is the site I used but there are many like this so use whatever site you prefer. For example's sake, you now have a list of over 315,000 contractors in hand with their phone numbers.

Now you want to put your ads in front of those 315,000 contractors that may or may not be on Facebook, so all we do now is upload that phone number list that you just scraped from the contractors list you bought, create a custom audience in the Facebook tool, and Facebook will go out and show your advertisements to that list of only phone numbers that are matching. That's got be by far the most targeted PPC on the planet right now.

What I'm trying to illustrate here for you is that you're looking at the most targeted opportunity with Facebook PPC. These are new doors, as far as marketing is concerned that has been opened for me and you both. As a matter of fact, we have never had such an amazing opportunity to place your ads in front of such a perfect audience. The beauty of this is, it's so easy and quick in today's world on Facebook.

And guess what? We just covered

Facebook strategies in the last few chapters. But there is still the option of advertising on LinkedIn and direct mail and a few other sources. But the reality is, you probably not going to need any of those other resources because Facebook alone is so powerful, plus remember we don't need that many customers to begin with.

So let's look at how we can get some of these customers because with the power of Facebook we really could never get in front get in front of them easier than you can today world. First thing is first is we generate leads. Let's look at this in more detail in the next chapter.

Part 9: Lead Generation the New Way

The lead generation methodology is by far the simplest marketing strategy ever to obtain new clients for your consulting business. Here is how it all works.

All you have to do is figure out what the most logical question your future prospects are going to be asking themselves, and you simply offer the question to their answer for free.

This is what's called a very compelling lead generation strategy versus convincing strategy. This is probably very different than what you typically are used to seeing out there.

Let's use a real-world example something that you're probably familiar with. Real-estate we have all lived in, rented, owned, bought and sold real estate at some point in our lives. This book is obviously not for us to discuss the topic of real estate but for the purpose of using a topic that we can all relate to let's use real-estate as an example, so let's look at real estate scenario, so we understand this strategy on a more detailed level.

So let's say you're a real-estate agent and you're looking for more leads, maybe you're looking for people that own really nice high-end ocean-front properties to have you as their real estate selling agent. Well, here is the strategy you use to do that.

The typical old way that you have probably encountered many times would be, you would create a full report, something like the "7 things you must know before buying ocean front properties." Then you would probably place that free report in from of that targeted audience as your way to generate leads. They would eventually request that report, and you would follow up with some sort of email chain.

This is the old way, and it worked pretty well, you would follow up with them, tell them how wonderful you are, some would probably agree to an appointment with you. Eventually, some would end up listing their house with you. After repeating this strategy a million times, you would have enough clients.

Now that we've looked at the typical old way of doing things, this was an example of a very typical strategy of convincing marketing; it's allot more push then pull marketing.

The new way of doing this is a whole another ball game. But before we get into more detail, about the new way of doing your marketing. Let's compare scenarios.

The reason you don't want to do it the old way would be, its screams salesman all day long. It's a very simple reason; you will not get such a great response because you have to convince them to pay attention to you, and your potential clients have seen that a million times before and they get it.

Now the right way to do this gives them a very obvious straight forward thing that your potential clients were looking for and all you do is to continue to help them until they are happy and they will continually ask you for further help in achieving their goals.

Let's look at a real world example of compelling marketing. We will re-visit the real-estate example we used earlier in this book. If me and you were partners, and let's say we own a lovely home on the ocean front somewhere on the Pacific coast. And we are now looking to sell that home.

So we agree that we are going to put it up for sale, split our profits and go out on a spending spree with our new earned profits from our house sale. The first question that will probably be on both our minds and that would probably be, what's the house worth, how much can we possibly get for our gorgeous oceanfront home? This would for sure be the most logical thought that we would have if we were looking to sell our home. I am sure our first thought would not be, who we can list it with?

I don't know about you but I know that I would be thinking "what can I get for my home " or "is this the right time to sell" or wonder if we can get allot of money for our home, maybe the real-estate bubble is still messed up, I am a bit worried, etc. We are going to say, 'Wonder what we can get for the place? Wonder if now! is the right time to sell? Wonder if we can get a lot of money for it? Maybe the real estate bubble is still messed up. I don't know. I'm freaked out!' These have to be the first questions going through your mind when you're going to sell. The most compelling offer that can be generated to get leads from guys like us selling ocean front properties would be to give away a free information on oceanfront home sales prices for 2017.

If me and my partner our selling our ocean front home, and the first question in our mind is what we can get for it, and we see an ad that says something along the lines of "selling your house here is a report of ocean front property prices in your area in 2017". Chances are very likely that I am going to respond to that ad because it's directly answering my biggest questions, and it's also very compelling.

The reason this is a superior method first is its non-douchey at all. Secondly, it has no evidence of having any commercial intent, thirdly it is attracting the people who are looking for that exact thing that you are offering, so it is always attracting the perfect clients. Fourthly, it is actually helping your potential clients achieve their goals; it's not just some fluff filled report that will not benefit them in any way, it has substance and fulfills what the client is exactly looking for at the moment, it also actually helps them out.

If you recall the formula for getting your possible clients to have confidence in you or your consulting service is what? Demonstrate that you can actually help them by actually providing the help. This is how compelling marketing works.

However, the final thing that it does is it also sets you up for the proceeding steps. Remember what we have done so far is generate leads, taken them to our opt-in page where they have requested our compelling report on ocean front home sales prices for 2017. Now that they are in our sales funnel they have seen that we are not douchey and that automatically sets us up for the next steps, which would be to get them to raise their hand and say to you, please help me, we need your help.

In the next chapter, we will look at how we do this in more detail.

Part 10: The 7 Step to Paying Customers

So they have opted into your opt-in page now what? Well let me show you the next seven steps to turn your prospects into paying customers, here is the 7 step process:

Step #1: Always offer your help for free: You should always start off by thanking your prospects for their interest and then giving a straight forward offer to help them for free, yes that means you don't charge them anything at this point.

Step #2: Explaining the Benefits, or how you can help them: Let them know in detail, how you can help them achieve their desired goals.

Step #3: Let them know why you're doing this: Your job is to answer that burning question in their mind by explaining in detail why you're offering to help in the first place.

Step #4: Eliminate their sales fear: Everyone

is going to be skeptical about you offering to consult for free, so it's your job to eliminate that fear.

Step #5: Create intrigue and irresistibility: You probably need to pay very close attention to this one because I am almost sure nobody has shown you this theory before.

Step #6: Remove non-selling

Step #7: Always get them to qualify: This is when they actually qualify themselves to you as prospects.

Now let's take a closer look at all these seven steps in more detail, so you understand how they work and how they fit into your consulting business strategy. Basically how you can put these steps to work in your consulting business.

Step #1: Always offer your help for free

This is the first step in your process, we always thank them for their interest, and then we offer to help them for free. The way this goes is, we will usually place our offer to help them in a sales letter, video, or PDF that we email these potential clients or even an audio format for them to listen to. The format does not really matter all that much. However video tends to be the most powerful in today's world, what is important is the message we get across to them. If we refer back to our real-estate example you should say something along the lines of "In this sales price report you'll notice that we have almost two identical homes sitting on the ocean front in your area. However, they have two dramatically different prices. Now would you like me to show you in detail why the one house sold for so much more money than the other home, and how we can get you the most money for your home also?" You see that's us offering to help them for free no charge.

Step #2: Explain the benefits, or How you can help them

Step number two is where we always explain the benefits of our help to our potential clients. This is where you would say something along the lines of: "I would be happy to help you put together a custom designed marketing plan for your house, identify your potential target buyers, and then show you how to present your property to them for its maximum price. With this marketing plan, you will be able to sell your house fast and get you the highest price without you wasting any of your time or money, and there is no cost or obligation of any kind. See what we just did here, we simply explained the benefits and the help that we would be providing for them.

Looking back you will see the following points:

- Identifying the perfect target market = benefit.

- A very custom marketing plan = benefit

- How to get maximum price possible plus present your home = benefit.

- Sell your house fast = benefit.

- Get you the highest price without you wasting your time or money = benefit.

So as you can see all I am doing is explaining the benefits. You don't have to give them a two-hour speech on all the benefits its simple, all you need is two Sentences explain the benefits that it. Nothing else is required.

Step #3: Let them know why you're doing this

Now as you may have figured out that your potential clients would be asking themselves or even you, why are you doing this for free? What's the catch here? What is going on?

Well, this is where you have to tell them in detail in no shady manner why we are doing this for them, this is where you do the unthinkable, and that's to be totally transparent with our marketing strategy. Using our real-estate example again you might want to say something along the lines of:

'I am a real-estate agent, and I am offering my service for free because and I sell ocean front properties exclusively. And there's a good chance that I possibly already have a buyer for your home, and considering that there is recent demand for oceanfront properties like yours. So if you have found value in my help so far, you might want to use me to sell your home.'

You notice we are not telling them how fabulous we are, we are simply coming clean as to why we are helping them. Nothing shady, just hey I am doing this for you because I am a realty agent. Because I'm a realtor right?"

Step #4: Eliminate their sales fear

Let's look at the fourth step in the process. Your potential clients still have that fear of the salesman, the consultant, and the marketer; they have the mentality to run for the hills. You will need to work with that; we need to eliminate the fear of the salesmen. Here's how we can do it in three simple sentences,

'With that said, please keep in mind I'm not offering you shady sales pitch in disguise. I promise not to ever pressure you in any way at all, as a matter of fact, if you feel like I have wasted any of your time...'

What we just did was eliminate the sales fear in the first two sentences.

As you can see we promised that we would not pester our client or pressure them in any way. We also promised that this wasn't a sales pitch in disguise as well. We are addressing these fears by doing this; we basically made them understand that this is not what this is. However, are they still going to be a little hesitant? Yes, of course, they will be! And that's where the next step in the process comes into effect.

Step #5: Create Intrigue and Irresistibility

Now, this next step in the process is extremely important. This part in the process is what I call the irresistibility and intrigue. In this step, we go back to our last statement to the client where we mentioned that "if you feel I have wasted any of your time" This is where we would insert a bribe of the sort. ...something along the lines of "I will write you a check for X amount of dollars, " or I will immediately market your home to thousands of potential buyers totally on my dime at no cost to you. Or even something like "I will cover all your realty fees." You need to make it completely irresistible to them.

Do you see how this is clearly irresistible to your potential clients? What your clients are probably thinking at this point is. This guy is offering me free help, and if I feel like my time has been wasted, he is going to give me money or do this stuff for free for me, so I have nothing to lose.

You see the irresistibility factor here? Not only does it provide massive amounts of intrigue, where your potential clients are probably thinking, that this guy is so confident, what in the world does this guy have to be so confident and such confidence in their ability to help me? But it also provides this massive intrigue where the person is saying 'This guy is so confident, what in the world kind of magical sauce can this person have to have that much confidence in their ability to help me?' When you are displaying that high level of confidence, it also instills a major increased confidence in you on their behalf as well; they are now intrigued, they are almost convinced at this point that you can help them to achieve their goals. So their interest level now is so much higher.

Step #6: Remove Non-Selling

Now this is where you start protecting your own self and what I mean by that is you start doing the takeaway, this can be a potent psychological trigger for your new clients. Now your potential prospects are thinking "ok I have nothing to lose here "at this point we are starting to take it away. We can now say something along the lines of '*wait a minute before you move forward, you should know that*

I can't help everybody. I can only really help or benefit people whose homes are directly on the oceanfront and in great sellable condition, and cannot be under foreclosure.'

Do you see where this is going at this point you are now listing criteria for them to qualify themselves to you, they must have this criteria in order for you to take them on as a client. Why would you want to do such a thing you're your clients? There are several very good reasons; number one it protects you from wasting your time with time-wasters. The second reason is it shows your clients that you are the last thing in the world besides being a shady salesperson. Your clients are not used to hearing, I cannot help everybody, I can only help certain clients, and I am only willing to work with only clients that meet my criteria. This is a very powerful psychological effect it has on your potential clients at this point. This now places you in the position of authority, and

> ## Its massive intrigue

they will start qualifying themselves to you.

Step #7: Always get them to Qualify

So here is the final step in this process, this is what we do next. Now you have already told them that you have certain criteria to take them on as a client, you have also made your offer irresistible, you have also built intrigue, but hers how you put it all together and phrase it.

This can be in a letter format or on your web page, pdf or even video You say, and again this could be in a letter format, on your web page, it could be a PDF or video; it doesn't really matter. It's the actual message that counts not the media format.

So here is what you would say, *'Here's what I would like you to do next. If you want to move forward schedule a planning session together with me, all you have to do is simply click the link below. When you click on my link, you'll see a form show up with a few questions about your property, and what you're looking to achieve. Once I have that information from you, then I will do some market research on your home, and we will set up a time to go over it together.'* When they go to your form and answer your criteria questions they are now qualifying themselves to you, do you see the picture now?

So what they are saying at this point is here is

the information on my home. Here is the condition my home is in, and here is how much I would like to sell my home for. Here is all the information that you asked for Mr. Realtor so you can decide on whether or not you should work with me. This is perfect reverse selling psychology 101.Let's review this process quickly if you go through the seven steps.

By the time you reach step number seven, you will have all these potential clients coming to your sales funnel, and the ones that actually make it through all the steps to step seven. What you end up with is a very much targeted group of responsive prospects who know exactly what you have to offer them, and they will be literally asking you to help them as soon as possible. They wouldn't be asking you for your help if they were not fully interested in becoming your client, just because you told them what you do. There is no guesswork; they know you're a realtor; you list houses, no surprises at this point.

Plus, these potential clients are essentially applying to speak with you too by answering all of your qualifying questions. Therefore you're protected from dealing with any time wasters or weirdos because you don't want your time wasted either, time is money for all of us.

So let's cover this in the next chapter.

Part 11: The Client Conversion System

You have now gotten to the point where you now have a nice list of potential clients who have already qualified themselves to you and are asking for your help to achieve their goals; they require your help immediately how do you convert them to paying clients?

Well, let's address that important question and look into how we will accomplish that. Here is how I approach this in my personal business, how it works in my specific business.

My personal prospects go through the similar irresistible intrigue process I explained to you earlier in this book. I offer them the ability to generate massive profits I always offer them $10.000 cash if I happen to feel like I wasted any of their time. And that's before they ever become one of my clients.

In the history of my business, I have never had a single individual request that I give them my

$10,000 because they felt I had wasted their time in any fashion. With such an offer like that of me risking my personal cash, I've really got to be on my game. So here's how I structure the deal. How I protect myself in this deal, so I don't get hosed.

So When they actually book an appointment to speak with me, they are asked to fill out a form with some simple straight forward questions like what's web site URL , what's size is your email list, how much in sales did they do last year, what sales goals do you have for this year, what their challenges are etc.

So I gather all this information just before I book anything or they request to speak with me.

Now, after I gather all this info on them I only schedule appointments with them whether on the phone, skype, or in some cases in person–only after I've carefully read their all their answers, really looked into them their business and thoroughly checked if I can indeed help them.

Before I even spend I minute of my time talking to my clients, I already have a very good understanding of how I am going to advise them.

I know already from checking them out whether or not they are a good match for me or not, they must already have the momentum that I require to help them before I move forward with them as clients, so I already know if I can help them or not.

That way there are no surprises when I actually speak with them, I already know who or what I am dealing with from the get-go. I already know at this point if they are a perfect match. So once we move onto that phone conversation, here is how I actually turn a prospect into a paying client. Again I call this the collaborative close.

So keep in mind that the people that I am talking to or you will be talking to, these people have asked you to call to call them.This is what I like to refer to as hot leads who need and want your help.

They have already answered all your questions; they have also already qualified themselves to you, there for at this point there is never going to be any sort of cold calls or sales calls of any kind. There are no surprises ever on the phone with your potential clients;

there is no funny business, I am not trying to teach you how to hard close anyone. All you are doing is genially getting on the phone and trying to help these people out.

When we close the sales with these clients whether it's on the phone or some other medium we actually do this by not selling, as strange as they may sound. We are actually using a process of generating new clients by anti-selling instead of the typical manner. Weird and different I know, but very effective.

Here is exactly how it is going to work. As I have mentioned earlier in this chapter, all you really have to do is demonstrate that you can actually provide your help by actually doing it for them , and then when your done offering to help them some more. Offer again.

I know this sounds like I keep repeating myself and it's very mundane, but in actuality, there is a very much a scripted structure that should be followed for this process to work for you. Let me explain and walk you through it.

PART #1: Collaborative Platform Building

Part one, Always start with collaborative platform building. We begin by asking your potential clients questions to find out want, and what their desired results are from working with you.

The one way I do this is like this, I say something like, 'Listen *John, If I was to have this conversation with you twelve months from now, what would make you happy if were looking back at your past year's results.*

What this creates in my potential clients is they start thinking twelve months ahead into the future picturing themselves working together with me, they will then start thinking of what they in vision as to what would need to happen for them to be happy with our working relationship and outcome.

This gives me a totally clear picture of where my new potential client wants to be. Next, what I will do is ask where he is at right now in his business goals, then I will ask a few more questions that lead to knowing more about what action he needs to take to achieve his business goals and where he wants to go with my help. After asking all my questions and getting all their answers, all I do is simply formulate a plan based on their answers and goals there looking to achieve. Does it sound complicated? I know can be a bit, but it will all make sense; let me explain a little further.

First I find out what point they are at with their business, where they would want to be, then after knowing these answers through my questions, I know have all the raw knowledge that I require to put together or form a plan. For the sake of clearing this process further, let's look at some example questions that I might ask potential clients to gather this raw information.

I would ask something like this 'Let's say me, and you were to work together for the next twelve months, what would need to happen in these twelve months working as a team for you to be happy?' And he says 'Well, I need to make at least 1.5 million dollars for the year. ' And I say 'Okay, well what are you doing presently per year now?' And he says 'I'm doing three-quarters of a million a year right now.'

So now that I know he is doing three-quarters a million a year – and he wants to be at a million and a half, now it's time to formulate that platform.

The next question that I may ask him would be something like 'Well, how many current customers are you getting per monthly basis right now?' And he probably gives me a number then I would say 'Okay, well, Now let me ask you this, do feel that there might be a bigger opportunity selling more products to your current customer base right now?

He might say something like 'Yes, actually allot of my customers are always asking for XYZ.' Then I would say 'Okay, well what do you feel that that your existing customers might like to purchase from you most right now?'

He might then say 'Well, my customers are buying my list building course, but they would really like to buy something that guides them on what to do once they have their database of prospects.' Now, do you see what is happening here I'm starting to get a visual plan from my client, we're working together building a plan as a team?

Then I might say 'Alright, what do you feel would happen if we offered this product to your customers do you feel that they would buy this product?' And they might say 'I definitely know some of them would buy it.'

'Alright great 'and then I usually ask more questions. 'So what exactly does your current sales process look like?' He would probably explain. And I'd say 'Alright, do you feel you would make allot more money at the point of sale if we added some click through upsells to your existing product.

He might reply with something like, 'Yes, I can see my orders increase from our point of sale transactions grow the monthly revenue that way.'

Then I will usually get into more detailed questioning like 'Ok what usually happens if your customers don't buy right away?' He might say 'usually not much, but they usually end up on our general list, and we send them an affiliate offer after several hours.'

Then I could say something like 'Ok, what do you feel might happen if we ran some sort of cash machine on automation to everyone who has not bought your product within the first 4 weeks of your sales funnel, and we offered a major discount on your product, what do you think would happen?'

They might say something like 'We actually tried something like that before, and we actually did really well, so I think it might get some good sales.'

You see where I am going with this and how my questions are framing a picture but yet I am not pushing my agenda on them, just asking questions, and asking them what they feel would happen if we tried my suggestions. What their ideas are around my suggestions.

Now that I am through with my process, and in my mind, I already have my bag of tricks. I am an online marketer, so I have a big bag of tricks or arsenal that I use. I have my four-day cash machine, email campaigns, one click upsell strategies and many other back-end strategies. So, once I'm through with this process, and now in my mind, I already have a bag of tricks. I am sure you also have your bag of tricks that your average client can benefit from.

So after analyzing everything I already know what bag of tricks I can use with this client. Maybe a bag of tricks sounds shady but in actuality in my tool set or my skill set that I use to service my clients and get them results, so there is nothing shady about it. Once I have put together my bag of tricks or formula for this client. I already know that this guy had run a sort of cash machine before and had some success, I also know that he could possibly create or sell another product and he can do some click up sales as well.

Part #2: Prescription Process

Once we gathered all this information from your clients now comes what I like to call the prescription process. Basically, we are creating a prescription to achieve their goals.

If you have noticed at no point during our conversation, I have actually told this person what to do. However, at this point, I will start prescribing activities to achieve their goals. Again as an example, I might say something along the lines of 'Based on what I know so far and what you have shared with me about your business, sounds like we should start offering XYZ product to your existing customers so we can generate immediate cash flow for you. Your client will probably say 'Yes, I think that would be a great idea.' I would then say 'It also sounds like a good idea to also run the four-day cash machine on all your unconverted leads that you may have. Your client then might say, 'Yes, I think that's what we spoke about earlier.' I would then say something like 'Ok going forward then, we could deploy someone click upsells so we can start seeing a spike in the amount of revenue you will be bringing in.

Part #3: Pre-close

Now, that I have the soft prescription in place, here is what I follow up with called a pre-closing question. I would ask something like the following, 'So tell me does that sound like an effective plan of action you can take to increase your revenue?' Do you see what I have done here? Basically, all I have done is just given all the answers he has given me, and created a plan of action steps out of them, and asked if it sounds like an effective plan for him?

Part #4: Final Closing

Now at this last step if the client says yes, then I use my final closing question. Are you ready for my big closing question? Here you go; my big hardcore close. I would say 'So would you like me to help you implement this plan going forward with your business?' I would say that 80% of my potential clients I speak with say yes.

My closing ratio is pretty good, out of ten clients I close at least 8 using this process 8 of them will say yes "I would like you to help me implement these strategies with my business, how do I sign up or become a client?"

This is how you do a collaborative close. That's a larger overview of how it's done. You don't have to act or be a typical sales person, nobody wants a shady salesperson or to be thrown a sales pitch. People just want to be helped they just want an easier path to their desired results. All you have to do is just demonstrate that you can actually help them, it's all pretty straightforward. Just help them, and your clients will sign up with you without much hesitation.

Part 12: Now is the Opportunity

We are now at the final chapter, and you're probably thinking that everything that we have gone through in this book sounds really easy, straight forward, it seems pretty obvious doesn't it? They can start a back-end sales process, of course, run the four-day cash machine, etc. Well, the reason it sounds easy to you because you're the consultant.

But in reality to your client it's not easy, they are not the experts at what you provide, and they don't see the easy picture as you see it. Your client sees this as a challenge and that's why they need your help. They are spending at least 40 hrs. A week or more on their business every day they simply don't have that same outside view as you have. It's not simple to them because they have to spend day in day out in the everyday grind of running the business and that in of itself can be a tremendous amount of a workload. Or whatever other activities they may do in their marketplace. You have the advantage as a consultant

The thing is, the very same methods that have been outlined for you in this book is exactly what I have used personally to run my consulting business every day. I have generated well over 100k a month whit this exact process and method, and that's only working part-time hours. As I stated earlier in this book my hours are usually from 8 am until about noon hour Monday through Friday. For me, I find it really easy and extremely fruitful return my time invested.

The bottom line is consulting is an extremely lucrative, fun, respectable and low stress service that you can provide that is simple to run as a business from anywhere in the world. You can offer it as a side business or as your full-time gig, now that's up to you, but now is the time

Now that we have gone through the entire process, the bottom line is if you are able to help other people achieve their business goals in a faster better way and you don't waste their time. If you can produce more revenue for them then, you have what it takes to become a successful consultant. As we covered earlier in this book, this is definitely one of the highest

109

paid professions on the planet right now doing approximately $100 billion in revenue a year according to Forbes magazine.

Consulting also happens to be one of the fastest growing industries in the world the stats show that its grown 83% just in the last few years according to the United States government , it's time to get your consulting practice up and running.

If you feel you have the skill set to help someone get much faster better results than they would if they did it themselves , then congratulations, you have what it takes to become a qualified consultant and your clients will be asking you for your help and asking to become one of you clients.

After reading this book you are now qualified if you take my advice and follow my steps and you work hard and intelligently, you are now qualified. If you are waiting for a diploma or being anointed as worthy, then you are going to be waiting for a long time maybe for life, take action get started and start making some big bucks. This business is out there for the taking and at the rate that it is growing the demand is out there, its huge jump in a get a piece of the action I can't emphasize this enough help other people and their businesses.

Start now, take action, and you will see great success. Take advantage of this incredible growing opportunity. You have the chance now to be a part of this $100 billion annual industry that is growing by leaps and bounds 83% just in the last few years when in reality there is no job security out there anymore, and it seems like the rest of the business world is not doing so well

People and their business need your help now more than ever before, and these huge numbers don't lie in regards to the demand out there. Consulting is growing by leaps and bounds ... this is your time, get in on it now!

People need your

help more than ever,

numbers don't lie